BIBLE STUDIES

INNER.LIFE

WELLBEING FOR HEART, SOUL AND MIND

BY TIM YEARSLEY

Navigators
UK

CONTENTS

WHY IS THIS WORTH YOUR TIME?

Have you ever struggled with your mental or emotional health? Have you ever known anyone that does? Have you ever wondered why the world is like this, and if things can be different? And have you ever found honest answers?

It might surprise you to know that the Bible speaks generously to these questions. The Bible's story makes it clear that to be human is to struggle with a broken world, broken people and our broken selves – but, more than that, it also tells us about a way of life that thrives, even in the midst of difficulty.

Christians believe they are a part of that story, and to be part of that story is to believe in a God who promises to renew us completely – mind, body, soul and strength – so that we might experience what life is really about, in all its joy, tragedy and triumph. No other ideology, philosophy or story paints such a beautiful picture.

And you're invited to be a part of it too.

WHERE'S IT GOING?

Inner.Life, the third in the *.Life* series, aims to connect the Bible's story with everyday reality.

The series is an attempt to think biblically about all of life. And some parts of 'all of life' can seem particularly difficult or confusing: work and rest, sex and relationships, mental health and wellbeing are all topics that we find ourselves wondering about, whether you would consider yourself a Christian or not.

After typing 'mental health' into the Bible Gateway website produced '0 results', what began as an investigation into a biblical perspective on mental health quickly raised further questions. For example, what do we even mean by 'mental health'? For many, it's now shorthand for 'mental *unhealth*'. If the Bible does not compartmentalise our 'health' in this way, how does it speak of the 'inner life' of a person, and what might that reveal to us that we may have missed?

Inner.Life is a journey through the biblical narrative, tracing through its pages the thread of what it means to be really, fully alive as God intended. It aims to wrestle with some of the very real questions related to mental and emotional challenges. But in exploring these issues, we will see how a biblical view of ourselves weaves together our heart, mind, soul and strength into a tapestry of humanness that God brings to life. 'Wellbeing', 'flourishing', 'peace' and 'shalom' are all descriptions of this kind of life – a life that is meant for a purpose: loving relationships with God, others, ourselves and the world. It is a life that can be experienced even in the midst of a broken world.

WHO'S IT FOR?

Inner.Life is for anyone looking to connect some theology to their (and others') experience of mental health and wellbeing. You don't have to be an expert! The studies won't point you to neat answers; rather they provide fuel for conversations around the questions that title each study. As such, context is more important than expertise: these studies would be best suited to mentoring relationships and small groups, which ideally would include a mature Christian or two who can share their wisdom with others.

They could just as easily form the basis for a teaching or seminar series. They aren't a substitute for professional treatment, however, and if you, or someone in your group, are struggling with mental illness, you should seek appropriate help. Your GP would be an excellent place to start.

HOW CAN YOU GET THE BEST OUT OF IT?

Honesty

What follows is not a story nor is it a self-help book, although we draw on real life stories and encourage you to think about the practical difference these studies will make. The studies themselves invite us to go deeper into the roots of our thoughts, feelings, desires and behaviours as we immerse ourselves in the Bible's story of our humanity. The more honest you can be, the better.

Patience

Just as physical health requires exercise, each study ends with an inner life 'exercise' – a practical way to work through the ideas from each set of questions. The aim of these exercises is to connect the 'theory' with some real life practice for the sake of experiencing, not just knowing, the truth. These exercises may take courage and some self-discipline but with patient practice they can be transformative.

Courage

Whether or not you would consider yourself a Christian should be no barrier to engaging with this material. Our conviction is that truth can stand up for itself, so rigorous and difficult questions are encouraged. But this isn't only truth to be believed in some abstract sense – it is truth that is beautiful and good. And beauty and goodness are to be experienced, so take courage, and be open to whatever might happen.

Preparation

These studies are also complemented by two talks (Change Your Mind part 1 and part 2) given at Navigators UK's Big Weekend 2018. You can find them at navigators.co.uk/resources/

These two talks are discussed in Study 7 but are particularly useful in giving an overview of the thinking behind this resource. If you are facilitating or leading others through these discussions or would like to get some background information, we recommend you listen to them before starting the studies.

A READING STRATEGY

Each study in *Inner.Life* follows the same pattern. The 'Starting from where you are' section begins with some thoughts from the author to kickstart your conversations (especially if you find yourselves asking 'where's he going with this?' at any point).

This section also offers a few questions to help you consider your own thoughts on the topic before opening up some extra input. Validating people's own journeys to this point is always a good place to start.

'Going deeper' is the meat of each study, and brings a section of the Bible into the conversation around the title question. Feel free to explore the Bible story or passage in your own way if the discussion needs it.

The 'Making it real' section is an opportunity to root the content of the discussion in some real world practicalities. It begins with a real life story of someone wrestling with the realities of being a Christian and facing mental health challenges. Take the time to read the story and, if in a group, consider if anything in the story resonates with anyone. The closing questions aim to tie the story into that study and to consider what real life applications can look like.

The final 'Getting practical' section is a suggested exercise that you can try out over the coming week. There is no obligation or expectation here, but should you, or a group of you, want to put the exercise into practice you are likely to have some significant experiences that can take you deeper into the truth and relevance of the Christian story.

In our road-testing of this resource we found that meeting to discuss each of the 11 studies weekly over a drink worked well. Reading through each study beforehand and jotting down your thoughts and answers in a journal will help you make the most of the discussions. Ultimately this resource is a tool that you can use in whatever way you think fits best. Add, subtract or modify the questions in each study as you see fit, although keeping the order of studies the same will help you enter into the biblical narrative more fully.

For a more thorough explanation of the flow of the studies, and thoughts that might be helpful to anyone leading others through them, you can download some notes for leaders at:
navigators.co.uk/inner.life-leadersguide

SO WHAT IS AN 'INNER LIFE'?

Although the research for this series began with questions around what the Bible has to say on the topic of 'mental health', it's important to clarify that the mind is not an easily distinct aspect of someone's inner life as far as the Bible is concerned.

In contemporary Western culture, the definition of the mind is often confined to our 'thoughts'. But both the Old and New Testaments use words we translate as 'the mind' alongside, and sometimes interchangeably with, words for 'the heart', 'the soul' and 'the body'. As such, it would be wrong for these studies to simplistically focus on the occurrences of the Hebrew/Greek words for 'mind'. Instead we hope to put the mind in the context of an understanding of our humanness that is multifaceted, integrated and purposeful.

It's not always easy to pull apart the distinct elements of our inner life since they are all interrelated and overlapping, but here are some helpful definitions:[1]

Our hearts – our feelings and emotions, our yearnings and longing, our capacity to love

Our souls – our distinctive personality, self-awareness and other-awareness

Our minds – our thinking, our rationality and determination, our understanding and judgement

Our strength – our bodies, the ability to live in this world, our energy and vibrancy, shown in our behaviours, all of which encases our heart, soul and mind

These aspects of us must be interconnected if we are to live well, and together we'll call them our 'inner life'.

[1]Adapted from Jamieson-Fausset-Brown Bible Commentary, Mark 12:30. biblehub.com/commentaries/jfb/mark/12.htm

WHAT ARE WE TALKING ABOUT WHEN WE TALK ABOUT AN 'INNER LIFE'?

STUDY #1

KEY IDEA

Our heart, soul, mind and strength are interconnected parts of who we are. Their purpose is to propel us into loving relationships with God and others.

KEY PASSAGE

Mark 12:28-34

'Love the Lord your God with all your heart and with all your soul and with all your strength' is a famous Hebrew command from the Old Testament (Deuteronomy 6:5).

In the New Testament, Mark writes in Greek and quotes the above verse, but he inserts an extra dimension: the mind. This is not an amendment to the command (the teacher of the law would have corrected Jesus if it were!) but rather Mark revealing a shade of meaning that might have otherwise bypassed the Greek readers.

The implication here is twofold. First, your mind is interconnected with the rest of your inner life. Since the Hebrew words for someone's 'heart' and 'soul' include what we (as inheritors of Greek philosophy) might think of as their 'mind', the Bible suggests that the heart, soul and mind are connected to each other, and together these are encased in our strength. In total, these add up to your 'inner life'.

Secondly, our inner life has a purpose. Part of what it means to be human is to be in pursuit of someone or something that we think will make life work. The command discussed in this passage suggests that the most important pursuit, the thing that really makes life work, is loving God and others with our whole being.

Q1 Up to this point in your life, how has what you believe affected your mental or emotional health?

Q2 How has your mental or emotional health affected what you believe (about yourself, others or God)?

Q3 What's been your experience of how someone's sense of wellbeing can affect their relationships, for better or worse?

Read Mark 12:28-34 in a couple of different Bible translations and note what strikes you from this conversation.

Q4 Why do you think the teacher of religious law asked his question?

Q5 Why do you think Jesus answered in the order that he did (God first and neighbour second)?

Q6 What do you imagine it looks like to love God with all of your heart, soul, mind and strength?

Q7 What do you think it means to love your neighbour as yourself?

Q8 Why do you think that these commands are more important than 'burnt offerings and sacrifices' (the religious duties of the time)?

Q9 What does this conversation between the teacher of religious law and Jesus imply about

(a) God?

(b) people?

(c) living life?

PRIYA'S STORY

I've had anxiety from quite a young age. My mum was really clean and tidy at home, and when I'd go for sleepovers at friends' houses I'd be anxious and worried about whether the food had gone off or whether the house was clean. At uni, when I was on my own out in the world, my anxiety got loads worse. I was having sustained intense panic attacks throughout the day. My memory of the first year was being in bed, surrounded by washing up, watching *Grey's Anatomy* and doing nothing, just asking myself: what kind of life is this? That and thinking about death, surrounded by paracetamol. But I didn't think I was unwell – and when I eventually got diagnosed with depression it was a word that made me feel sick and dirty. I struggled to tell people this was what was going on with me. It just carried on for about two years.

It was really physical, which is probably why I didn't think it was a mental health issue. My symptoms were similar to having food poisoning – stomach cramps, sickness, running to the toilet. I'd look forward to a party that evening, but the dread of going would grow until I'd end up in bed not going out. I was really lonely.

What helped most was having a key friend in my life with whom I could be totally honest about the state of my mind and not worry about the consequences on the relationship. All this dark stuff in me needed to be gotten out in the presence of someone who would listen and say, 'That's OK' – that was massive. Not for them to try and fix it, but to be OK with it and show me they loved me anyway.

I'm better now than I ever could have imagined being. I'm functioning. I've got a Masters degree. I manage to drive to work every day and be on time. I have healthy relationships. I do fun things. I know that I'm valuable and loved. I still feel like I have a depressive personality – even though I get excited and love people and things, they still feel like objective descriptions rather than genuine emotions. But, a good life isn't one that is really happy all the time. It's about richness and sometimes this has to be worked for.

Q10 What do you notice about how the different parts of Priya's inner life related to each other (and her outer life – her relationships and the world around her)?

Q11 If our inner life is made up of these overlapping parts (heart, soul and mind within strength), what are the implications for how we think about what it means to be a healthy person?

Q12 Reflecting on all of this study, what motivates you to pursue a healthy inner life?

This week you could try practising the art of the 'Examen'. This is a well-known spiritual exercise that helps people grow in self-awareness of the parts of each day that have drawn them closer to God, as well as those parts that have distanced them from God. It has five steps, but you can build up to attempting all five.

STEP 1

Be still and ask God to give you clarity and understanding

STEP 2

Be grateful for the day

STEP 3

Look back over your day and pay attention to moments when you felt close to God, and moments when you didn't

STEP 4

Look in to a moment that stands out and pray it through

STEP 5

Look forward to tomorrow and ask God for his help

Why not take 10 minutes each day this week to go through the Examen?

It can be helpful to keep a journal and it is often fascinating to see patterns emerge over time.

WHAT WERE GOD'S ORIGINAL INTENTIONS FOR OUR MINDS?

STUDY #2

KEY IDEA

At our core, we are created well by a good God who designed us for relationship.

KEY PASSAGE

Genesis 1:26-2:25

We all know that the world is a broken place. We see evidence of it every day, not only on the news, but in the messiness of our own lives and relationships. It's easy to agree that things shouldn't be like this. But how *should* they be?

The opening chapters of the Bible describe the good world that a good God created. It's important to understand that this world was once full of beauty and potential (even if we only hear echoes of that now). We can cling on to the truth that people are loved by God, even if they don't recognize it. We can resist the pull of cynicism and complacency that says, 'This is just the way it is'. And we can know that our minds were created to be good and to do good as an expression of love for our Creator.

Q1 What contributes to your sense of self-worth?

Take some time to read Genesis 1:26-2:25 and note what strikes you, what you like or dislike, and where you have questions.

Q2 What are some of the implications of God creating us in his image and likeness (Genesis 1:26-27)?

Q3 What kind of intentions do you think God had for Adam and Eve's

(a) inner life?
(b) relationships (with God and others)?
(c) purpose?

Q4 How do you think all these things (from Q3 and Q4) combined to give Adam and Eve a sense of self-worth?

Q5 Read Psalm 139:13-18. What are the implications of the idea of 'the image of God' for the way we see

(a) ourselves on a good day?
(b) ourselves on a bad day?
(c) people we like?
(d) people we don't like?

Q6 From all the above, how do you understand God's original intentions for our inner life?

To be made 'in the image of God' is a mysterious and deep part of being human. Though our human experience falls a long way short of God's intentions for us, there is nowhere in the Bible that speaks of the image of God ever being lost (in fact quite the opposite – see Genesis 9:6 and James 3:9). This is huge. It means that, despite all our shortcomings, all people carry God's image. It means that you are made in God's image. And it means that no amount of brokenness you experience can ever diminish your worth.

NAOMI'S STORY
(PART 1)

Before I got ill, no one ever taught me about mental 'health'. As a teenager I self-harmed. I regarded myself as depressed. I would just cry. I would lock myself in my room and hate everything around me and think that everyone around me hated me. I attempted suicide when I was 15. My mum's suggestions like exercise, therapy, and not being alone too often were good suggestions, but these were more like sticking plasters because they didn't get to the root issues that caused everything. On a surface level I coped up until university, but I was building on a broken foundation.

At one point, God gave me a picture of cleaning a broken vase. And then another image was of him dropping the vase. The broken foundation of my life needed to go. Going through the 'I am' statements in Paul's letter to the Ephesians – I am holy, I am loved, I am forgiven – was huge for me, and it changed how I viewed myself and my decisions.

I think I might still be depressed. I still cry a lot about my life. But even in that not coping well, I don't feel out of control. I still struggle with deep lies and an inability to see people's love for me. But it just doesn't affect me as much because I know that's not how God feels and that doesn't hold my worth. I can have bad days and if I'm not sleeping I can't complete the same tasks, but it doesn't mean I'm less worthy because my worth isn't tied to that.

Knowing that this is not how God created us gives me hope. Adam and Eve were completely shame free and open and vulnerable. Jesus gives us that opportunity again. Revelation 21 talks about how God will wipe away every tear. There will be no more pain and suffering that can't be coped with, and we won't be lonely anymore. We suffer in our separation from Jesus right now – but there is hope in the midst of that suffering. I know this isn't the best it can be because God is not fully present. Being reunited is God's plan and his intention from the beginning.

Q7 Where do you see a sense of self-worth coming from in Naomi's story?

Q8 If you consider yourself to be made in the image of God, what happens?

This week you could try 'soaking yourself' in the words of some Hebrew poetry. Specifically, try Psalm 139. Set a timer for a few minutes each day, ask God to speak to you, and read the psalm through. Pause now and then, to think about it with your heart, soul, mind and strength. Also, read the psalm in different translations, listen to it on audio, read it aloud. See what stands out to you each day, and at the end of the week pause to reflect: what difference would this make to my life if I lived as if it were true?

WHY DO WE STRUGGLE?

STUDY #3

KEY IDEA

The Fall fractures our inner life and our relationships. We adopt flawed solutions that do not address the deeper problems.

KEY PASSAGES

Genesis 3
Jeremiah 2:13

The story of Adam and Eve in the Garden ends with tragedy and pain. Their intimate relationship with God and each other is in tatters as they hide themselves. Their sense of security and self-worth is shattered as they irrationally lash out and divert blame from themselves. Fig leaves seem like a woefully poor attempt to deal with the problem.

Many centuries later, the prophet Jeremiah speaks out God's words to God's people, who were in exile at the time. Though he was speaking into a specific context, Jeremiah's words capture the predicament of all humanity outside of Eden. First, we have left God behind – the true source of life, health and self-worth. And secondly, rather than running back to him and asking for his mercy and help, we are addicted to our own solutions despite their inability to do the job. Just like Adam and Eve's fig leaves, we grab onto things to help us get by without really dealing with the underlying causes of our problems.

Q1 Have there ever been times in your life when you have struggled with mental or emotional health? What did this look like? You could think in terms of your thoughts, feelings, desires or behaviours.

Read Genesis 3 and note what strikes you, what you like or dislike, and where you have questions.

Q2 What is the serpent's strategy for tempting Eve?

Q3 What significance do you see in Adam and Eve's realisation of their nakedness? And how does this compare with the last sentence of Genesis 2?

Q4 There is a fracture in their relationships. What can you learn about the consequences of Adam and Eve's eating the fruit from their responses to God and his questions?

Q5 How do the consequences that God pronounces affect Adam and Eve's

(a) inner life?
(b) relationships (with God and others)?
(c) purpose?

You may like to compare your answers to those for Q4 of Study 2 and think about how this fracturing takes hold.

PETE'S STORY

It's in the background so it becomes a part of normality which makes talking about it difficult. For me actually my OCD [obsessive-compulsive disorder] is a coping mechanism that, at least in the beginning, was a fairly good thing. When I was a teenager I had a rough time with friends, but the overanalysing turned into obsessing and it became its own relief. Stress brings it on now, and OCD helps me feel better for a time, but spending 2-3 hours on this rather than the thing that is actually the problem can be destructive and counter-productive.

I'd write, see I'd written something, then obsess over two sentences for hours. A resolution to kill the obsessions helped me get from writing a couple of sentences to about 700 words a day routinely. I also had chronic fatigue. I had a year out, but it didn't really help until I asked an old friend from university to start asking me about it every week. Before that I was despairing because I had these conditions and it was all-consuming. My friend talked about this being a thorn in the flesh; sometimes these get better and sometimes they don't. But it is worth talking about.

Right now, I still have the same problems, although the scale and scope has changed. Being honest with the right people, who themselves are understanding and accepting but not mollycoddling, is helpful. My own coping mechanism is to have routine, as planning is a good thing for chronic fatigue. I'm trying to build my life on the Bible. Here are purposes and a measure of what is right. Having a routine and a plan to get on with gives me direction.

Q6 Where do you see the evidence of relational and internal fracture in the world around you, or in Pete's story above?

Q7 Where do you see evidence of relational and internal fracture in your own life?

Q8 Consider these words from Jeremiah 2:13 (The Message)

'Stand in shock, heavens, at what you see!
Throw up your hands in disbelief – this can't be!'
God's Decree.
'My people have committed a compound sin:
they've walked out on me, the fountain
Of fresh flowing waters, and then dug cisterns –
cisterns that leak, cisterns that are no better than sieves.'

What 'cisterns that leak' (flawed solutions) are you tempted to use?

Q9 How well do you think the story in Genesis 1-3 helps us understand the world we live in?

Q10 Jesus acknowledges the fracturing and striving we all feel when he says, *'Come to me, all you who are weary and burdened, and I will give you rest'* (Matthew 11:28). What does this promise mean to you?

The world is full of promises that offer to alleviate the pain of living outside the Garden, alienated from God, one another and ourselves. This week you might like to practise attentiveness as an exercise in exposing some of the 'cisterns that leak' around us. Consider the following quotation from The School of Life's *How to Reform Capitalism*:[2]

'Adverts wouldn't work if they didn't operate with a very good understanding of what our real needs are; what we truly require to be happy. Their emotional pull is based on knowing us eerily well.'

As you go about your day-to-day life, look out for claims that tell us how we can really experience life, health and self-worth. Do you find them appealing? Keep track and share your experiences next time you meet.

It might be helpful to write out Matthew 11:28 and carry it with you throughout the week. It will give you a constant reminder of God's perspective as you study the world's perspective.

[2]The School of Life (2017) *How to Reform Capitalism*, p. 61. London: The School of Life.

WHAT DOES A HEALTHY INNER LIFE LOOK LIKE?

STUDY #4

KEY IDEA

Jesus shows us what a beautiful inner life in action looks like: to be in tune with our thoughts, emotions and desires, not mastered by them.[3]

KEY PASSAGE

John 11

[3] Find out more at desiringgod.org/articles/jesus-is-fully-human.

The idea that God became a man has mind-boggling implications for how we think about what it means to be human (let alone what we think about who God is). In explaining Jesus on earth, theologian John Calvin wrote, 'Christ has put on our feelings along with our flesh'.

Jesus had a body, emotions, a mind and desires. In taking on all these aspects of our humanness, Jesus was and is 'the image of the invisible God' (Colossians 1:15).

This means at least two things. First, God endorses our humanity. Our body, emotions, thoughts and desires are all valid parts of what it means to be human, of what it means to be created in the image of God.

Secondly, Jesus models for us how these aspects of our humanness can add up to something – the kind of life that is purposeful in its love for God and others.

Q1 Which of the following are you most likely to trust: your thoughts, your emotions, your desires, or your behaviour? What are the benefits and drawbacks of leaning on each?

Take some time to read through the story of Jesus and the death of Lazarus in John 11. Note what resonates and what jars, and where you have questions.

Q2 Who are the characters in the story and what do you imagine drives them?

Q3 Why do you think Jesus answered Martha in the way he did?

Q4 Why do you think Jesus responded to Mary in the way he did?

Q5 Which facets of Jesus' inner life are on display in this story? (You could think in terms of his thoughts, emotions, desires and behaviour, or his 'heart, soul, mind and strength'.)

Q6 If Jesus already knew how this story would end, why do you think he experienced the emotions that he did?

Q7 How do you think Jesus allowed his thoughts, emotions, desires and behaviour to influence him but not master him? Based on this passage, how did he find the strength and ability to remain balanced?

Q8 How do you think the various characters would have felt towards Jesus by the end of this story?

AVA'S STORY
(PART 1)

On paper, things were good: graduating, getting married, first house, Dave's job. So why was I so disconnected from that and feeling crap all the time? It took a long time to realise it wasn't normal. I was having more panic attacks, but I didn't seek help until Dave and his parents sat down with me our first Christmas together and suggested it.

Flash forward to seeing a GP and being told that this was a real thing, not that I wasn't strong enough to deal with it – that was a breakdown moment. Before that I was kind of aware of it, but I just didn't care. It crept up slowly… I felt crap today became I felt crap all month. It took people saying to me 'This isn't who you are' when I was exhausting myself trying to look fine. People are getting better at noticing this in me, even though it's taken me a long time to accept other people's help because I wanted to convince myself I was OK.

I've realised that I'm still allowed to feel sad sometimes – that's a legitimate emotion. Having open and honest conversations with people has really helped. If my anxiety is really bad, everything is cranked up to 11. With depression, it's a lack of anything, a flatness. They're tangled up with legit concerns or sadnesses, and often hindsight is the only way to tell them apart and see the patterns. I can think hopefully about the future right now, instead of being in an endless dark tunnel.

Having good mental health allows you to experience a whole range of emotions. Sadness, anger, fear, etc. might be seen as 'bad', but we lose a lot of human experience if we can't legitimately feel and experience them. Bad mental health is the inability to experience those! Not everything is great all the time, but in the bad things you can experience peace, and feeling sad makes you appreciate what is good. Coming out of bad patches of depression makes me cling on to the small things, like the people I depend on to keep going. I appreciate every anniversary I have with Dave because he's still there. There's no such thing as perfect physical health and likewise with mental health. But why would I want to give up all the good things I have?

Q9 Ava talks about how our inner life can run deeper than we realise. What might stop you from exploring the depths of your own inner life?

Q10 What do you make of Ava's desire to feel negative emotions as well as positive ones?

Q11 Although much of our inner life exists below our consciousness, we can trust that God sees every part of us (beautifully captured in Psalm 139). How might you take steps to become more aware of the different parts of your inner life, and give voice to those parts?

The story of Jesus and Lazarus is a powerful way to explore what it means to live well in the midst of broken circumstances. Yet stories often go one of two ways – they show us what it means to go on a journey towards being fully human, or they tell cautionary tales that warn us of what it would be like to descend into a less-than-human life.

Films are also powerful stories. You might like to watch one this week and discuss it with these questions in mind:

- Which characters become fully human and which ones become less than human?

- Is the film's portrayal of full humanness (or less-than-humanness) something you agree with?

Here are some films about characters who wrestle with their 'inner life':

- *A Beautiful Mind (2001)*
- *A Monster Calls (2016)*
- *The Intouchables (2011)*
- *Inside Out (2015)*
- *Manchester by the Sea (2016)*
- *Limitless (2011)*

If you are not a film-lover, perhaps read a book or write a short story to explore these ideas. Or just sit in a café and watch the people around you. Every person has a powerful story.

HOW IS CHANGE POSSIBLE?

STUDY #5

KEY IDEA

Repentance is something we often resist but it's really about acknowledging we need help and opening ourselves up to God.

KEY PASSAGES

Luke 5:27-32
Psalm 51

The two things I resent most in life are DIY and getting sick. What's the link? As long as I feel like I can do something about my problems, then I'm in control, I can fix it, and I don't need help. But both DIY and illness bring me face to face with my own limitations; they force me to recognise that I don't have what it takes. And even more painfully, that I need help.

But my wife tells me that's a good thing. It's forcing me to realise that depending on myself holds me back from experiencing what life is really about. It is throwing myself into loving relationships with God and others where I can both give and receive love, encouragement and support. The psychologist Dan Allender captures this idea as he explains what repentance is really about:

'Repentance is an internal shift in our perceived source of life. It is recognising that our self-protective means to avoiding hurt have not ushered us into real living… or to purposeful, powerful relating. Repentance is the process of deeply acknowledging the supreme call to love, which is violated at every moment, in every relationship.'[4]

More and more, I'm realising not only what repentance means, but what it makes possible. When I hold up my hands and say 'I don't have what it takes… I need help', it isn't an act of weakness, it's an opportunity for God and others to step in.

Q1 What responsibility do you think someone should take for the state of the own inner life? In particular, for

(a) their condition?
(b) their conduct?
(c) their coping mechanisms?

[4] Dan B. Allender, *The Wounded Heart*, p 199 (NavPress, 2008)

Spend some time immersing yourself in the story of Jesus at Levi's house, found in Luke 5:27-32. Who was this man? What's the atmosphere? Who are the characters? What strikes you from this story?

Q2 Apparently, Levi's life seems sorted. Why do you think he was so quick to follow Jesus and then invite Jesus to his home?

Q3 Why do you think some people felt the urge to complain about who Jesus spent time with?

Q4 Jesus says, '*I have not come to call the righteous, but sinners to repentance.*' Why do you think Jesus said this to someone who on the outside appeared all together?

Q5 The Greek word for repentance – *'metanoia'* – means a change of mind, a change in the inner life. How does this help you understand what Jesus wanted for Levi?

Read Psalm 51:1-4.

Q6 Why do you think David wrote this psalm?

Q7 What does David hope for from God and what changes would this bring to his inner life?

CHRIS' STORY

Although I've never been diagnosed with depression, I do have times when I get depressive thoughts ('I'm not good at this' or 'People don't like me'). They're not true but you can't get rid of them. A pattern would be that I felt sad and let the negative thoughts win, because they are so pervasive. You can end up believing them because you keep hearing them. I'd retreat, isolate myself from people. And then THAT would make the statements come true. 'Oh look, nobody does care, nobody likes me.' When I'm feeling like that now though I try and busy myself, surround myself with people, go for coffees, attend events. The worst thing for me is to hide away.

Feeling darker thoughts can be a bit like fumbling around in a dark room grabbing whatever is near you. I could see the light and I knew there was help there, but in the light I would see myself. And that was scary. I wanted to believe in myself, that I could fix it. Eventually things got to a point where I came to realise the unifying factor in all the bad situations I was in: it was me.

Sometimes people don't want to get out of the bad moods. It's something you can blame. If things aren't going well it's not because of me, it's because of the bad mood. That is a friction or a barrier to recovery from depression/mood disorders. If I do recover I won't have something to attribute my faults and flaws to… so I have to

actually face myself. This is scarier and more difficult, it takes more effort. Everyone wants to improve themselves, unless that actually involves changing.

So where does God fit in? When you go through mood disorders it can be very isolating and you feel like no one can help. But that's not necessarily true. For me, the way that God helps is being alone and thinking about how good God is and the way he loves me – even though that's difficult because it also leaves space for the darker thoughts to come in again. Praying and spending time with God in the Word does help you forget the darker thoughts; it occupies your mind.

Q8 Chris talks about blaming his bad moods, and the fear of facing up to himself. To what extent does this resonate with your own experience?

Q9 Often willingness to change only comes when the pain of staying the same gets too great. How might a posture of repentance (see your answer to Q6) help that process come about?

Q10 Having discussed all of the above, would you answer the first question in this study any differently?

'Confession' is a loaded word for many people but at its root it simply means to 'acknowledge'. Building a rhythm of confession into life can be a helpful way to acknowledge that there are things we get wrong, times we look for love and life in the wrong places, and opportunities to ask for help that we bypass. Confession keeps our feet on the ground and stops us believing our own hype.

Importantly, it is always met with the promise of forgiveness and healing from God – sometimes found as we read the Bible, sometimes heard from the mouths of others, and sometimes felt deep within us. Confession is a practice that encourages repentance and the new start that comes with it.

You might like to revisit the practice of the Examen outlined in Study 1. Or maybe you could consider whether there is someone in your life whom you trust enough to practice confession with this week, and in the weeks to come? All you need is the courage to pray the words of David from Psalm 26:2:

'Test me, Lord, and try me, examine my heart and my mind.'

WHAT DIFFERENCE DOES THE CROSS MAKE?

STUDY #6

KEY IDEA

The cross is God's decisive intervention into our broken world: Jesus died the death we should have died so we can live the life we were meant to live.

KEY PASSAGE

Luke 23:32-43

Q1 Can you think of an example (fictional or real) in which a character sacrifices themselves to save others? What happened?

Q2 What emotions did this evoke in you?

The cross is the catalysing force in God's rescue plan. It is mysterious but it is beautiful. God himself feels the full brutality of a broken world: an innocent man chooses the death penalty on our behalf. It gives us a foothold to understand how a loving God deals with suffering.

Consider this: if God is made up, then suffering exists as a fact of life – even a way of life – and it needn't provoke us to cry out, 'Why?' The universe is just blind and indifferent. But that's a pretty bleak outlook on life that doesn't sit comfortably with most people. Actually, the fact that we feel pain and brokenness in ourselves and all around us points to the sense we all have that this world is not as it should be. Don't we want someone to do something about it?

Moreover, what if God is not just sitting idly by, observing pain and suffering from a distance? What if he too longs to end suffering? Perhaps he has even done something about it…

The cross is a picture of a loving God who takes the full force of evil on our behalf. Jesus Christ hanging on a cross, making a way for people to know the God who loves them and wants to heal them.

Read Luke 23:32-43.

Q3 What strikes you on first reading? Why?

Q4 Look more closely: some characters are mocking Jesus. What do you think their reasons are?

Q5 Do you think Jesus *could* have saved himself? Why or why not?

Q6 What contrasts do you notice between the first and second criminal (especially in regards to the state of their 'inner life')?

Q7 The second criminal asks, '*Jesus, remember me when you come into your kingdom*' (v 42). What do you think he means, and what does this reveal about him?

Q8 What do you make of Jesus' promise to the second criminal, and why do you think he said this?

Q9 What do you think happened next?

Q10 Peter, one of Jesus' closest friends and disciples, wrote the following:

'*When they hurled their insults at him, he did not retaliate; when he suffered, he made no threats. Instead, he entrusted himself to him who judges justly. "He himself bore our sins" in his body on the cross, so that we might die to sins and live for righteousness; "by his wounds you have been healed."*'
(1 Peter 2:23-24)

What do you think Peter is saying about why the cross matters so much for humanity?

KATY'S STORY
(PART 1)

This issue probably started earlier than I realised, like around Year 12. I was really tired all the time, not sleeping properly, not eating properly, not feeling happy, not working properly or feeling like I could. I probably had depression, but my school was focused on my work output rather than my wellbeing.

University wasn't as bad as I'd worried. Halfway through the first term I became a Christian, which turned everything upside down. At the end of the first term I had my first panic attack.

The first time I lent on God with this, I was feeling really twitchy and itchy like I needed to self-harm. Didn't know why. I texted a friend and he texted back Philippians 4:4. I read it, prayed, instantly felt better. It was immediate. Praying that I didn't want to feel like this formed quite a lot of my prayers, asking God, 'Why do I feel like this?'

My journey with my mental health has been a big part of my journey with God. I have a much wider group of people who are around me and know the real me. As I've got more comfortable and confident in my identity with God, I am more willing to show people who I really am. It used to be, 'Yeah, I'm a Christian but I'm still the same person', but now it's like, 'This is who I am now, this is who I am with Jesus and this is what he does for me'. I was anxious people wouldn't get that, but people are more and more receptive.

Jesus is changing me and healing my pain, and that's someone worth following and loving.

Q11 How easy do you find it to believe that Jesus' death on the cross can affect someone in the here and now, like in Katy's story?

Q12 If all of this is real, what difference could it make to you?

The story so far has been rich: God created a good world full of very good people. But humanity is tempted to go their own way… and does. 'Cisterns that leak' abound as we scrabble around trying to find a way back to wholeness, each other and God. But only those that acknowledge they need help have a chance of finding it. So God himself takes centre stage in humanity's story and makes a way for us to find life the way it was always meant to be lived: in purposeful, powerful, loving relationship with him, each other and our very selves.

Take a moment to hold that story in your mind. Does it make sense? Does it explain the way the world is? Does it make sense of what we long for?

If you're considering this story afresh, or for the first time, as a story that rings true, then you can respond to God in a personal way. Could you even pray the following prayer?

God, if it's possible to have a relationship with you, then I want to know you. I don't want to just believe what other people say is true about you, but I want to know who you really are and the way this world really is. I believe that Jesus died to heal me and this world: so show me how I can be healed from the inside out, and start that work in me. Please help me step into the life you have in store for me. Connect me with others who want to do the same.

Before next time: Listen to the two talks given by Ros Boydell at the Navigators UK Big Weekend 2018 (if you only have time to listen to one, dive straight in at the second). You can find them at navigators.co.uk/resources/.

HOW CAN I FIND HEALING FOR MY MIND?

STUDY #7

KEY IDEA

The Holy Spirit takes us beyond coping mechanisms to inside-out transformation.

KEY PASSAGE

Romans 8

On 8 June 1978, Aleksandr Solzhenitsyn, the gulag survivor and Nobel prize winner, gave a famous address to students graduating from Harvard. He said, 'If humanism were right in declaring that man is born only to be happy, he would not be born to die... [His purpose] has to be the fulfilment of a permanent, earnest duty so that one's life journey may become an experience of moral growth, so that one may leave life a better human being than one started it.'

To believe in Christianity is to believe in much more than a coping mechanism. It is a belief that 'moral growth', as Solzhenitsyn puts it, is empowered transformation from the inside out. Christianity isn't a bandage to cover over a wound, but heart surgery that reintegrates all of who we are. Our hearts, souls, minds and bodies no longer have to compete with each other for mastery over us. Christians have a new master – we are governed by the Holy Spirit, Jesus Christ, God himself, living in us.

Which means that if you have the Spirit, you can claim the supreme promise that in all things, God works for our good so that we might look more like his son (Romans 8:28-29). And that means an inner life just as God intended it to be in the Garden - not fractured or contradictory but integrated back into wholeness. It's the kind of life that we always longed for but never knew how to find.

Q1 What's your reaction to the Solzhenitsyn quotation above?

Q2 How do you think most people go about obtaining the 'moral growth' he describes?

Q3 What did you make of the talks (particularly talk 2) by Ros Boydell at the Big Weekend 2018?[5]

Take some time to chew on Romans 8:1-8 with an eye on how Paul understands the role of the Holy Spirit in bringing about some of the things Solzhenitsyn aspired to.

Q4 What strikes you?

Q5 How would you summarise the main idea in a sentence?

Q6 What are the implications for you of living with 'no condemnation' (v 1)? How might life be different?

Q7 What reasons does Paul give for us needing the Holy Spirit?

Q8 What does the imagery of having a mind 'governed' by the Spirit bring up for you (v 6)?

Q9 Look forward in the chapter to verses 18-30. Does anything here in the language of 'waiting' or 'groaning' resonate with your experience?

Q10 What do the promises that Paul sets out at the end of this chapter mean to you?

[5] If people weren't able to listen to the talk in advance of this week, then take the time now to listen and respond to it together. The questions that follow can help you go deeper if you have time.

KATY'S STORY
(PART 2)

At university, I started meeting up with a friend who forced me to process my depression and anxiety. It was chaotic working through this stuff as well as all the normal uni stuff of working out who I was, as well as just becoming a Christian.

What I'd been unconsciously doing was putting my identity in my anxiety and using it as a crutch. It was anxiety inducing to think about life *without* anxiety because I'd built in coping mechanisms and I wasn't sure who I'd be without it. But simultaneously I had the realisation that I could let go of this. God was asking me to let it go and give it to him. So I did.

I was lying across the chairs in the uni chapel and wrestling this through: 'Do I want to see who I am without this?' I didn't want to keep being the person I was – someone who finds buying enough pasta and choosing the right cheese anxiety inducing. I'd been

praying pretty much since day one, but I had to realise how unfunctioning I'd become. I got to the place where the pain of staying the same was greater than the pain of changing. I immediately felt free.

I'm still on medication and going to therapy but feeling lighter and better. I suddenly have all this time in my day. I am closer with God and can talk to him about everything. God's acceptance has been key. I don't need to be perfect. I feel loved for who I am. I know he's always there for me. He is a solid foundation for my identity.

Q11 Check out Galatians 4:4-7. What does this mean to you?

Q12 How does Katy's story illustrate the ideas in the Galatians passage?

Q13 In light of this study, is there anything you need to start believing? Is there anything you need to stop believing?

In Luke 11:11-13, Jesus says, *'Which of you fathers, if your son asks for a fish, will give him a snake instead? Or if he asks for an egg, will give him a scorpion? If you then, though you are evil, know how to give good gifts to your children, how much more will your Father in heaven give the Holy Spirit to those who ask him!'*

This is one of those passages that seems hard to reconcile with a view of Jesus as a nice moral teacher, especially when Jesus calls people evil. We sit up and take notice. But the point he makes is even more shocking than the language he uses to make it: *God wants to give his Holy Spirit to anyone who asks him.*

Is there anything holding you back from asking God for his Holy Spirit to come into your inner life? Could you ask him to begin to heal you, so that you might experience his love and help? Could you ask him this week?

HOW CAN I LIVE IN THE DIRECTION OF A (RE)NEW(ED) ME?

STUDY #8

KEY IDEA

If our identity is rooted in God's love, then we express this through worship. Worship is about reorienting the trajectory of our lives and gives us (re)new(ed) purpose.

KEY PASSAGE

Romans 12:1-2

Q1 How might the health of our inner life be affected by any of the following?

(a) our physicality
  (our environment and our physical health)
(b) our social life
(c) our spiritual life
(d) our psychology

No one seeks out boredom. In fact, most people fill their lives with things that help them avoid it at all costs. This might sound crazy, but pressing into our fear of boredom can reveal some deep things. Why do we feel uncomfortable or restless? Is my boredom showing me things about me that I'd rather not confront? Is there a fear that an underlying nothingness or 'meh' is the bedrock of my life?

In *The Anxiety & Phobia Workbook*,[6] Edmund Bourne writes the following:

'All the techniques described so far can help a great deal, yet for certain people they aren't quite enough. An underlying level of anxiety remains – an anxiety that comes from not having answered basic questions about the meaning and purpose of your life... ['Existential anxiety'] arises from feeling held back...from being all that you can be.'

Q2 To what extent do you agree with the quotation from *The Anxiety & Phobia Workbook*, that there can be a deeper, 'existential' reason for our struggles?

[6]Edmund J. Bourne, *The Anxiety & Phobia Workbook*, p 19 (New Harbinger, 2015)

Q3 How might this deeper cause be an outworking of the consequences of living outside of the Garden? (It may help to look back to your conclusions from Study 3.)

Q4 The writer Henri Nouwen insightfully points out that we often define ourselves according to our answers to one of three questions: 'What do I do?', 'What do others say about me?' and 'What do I have?' Which of these are you tempted to use to define yourself?

Q5 Another writer, Brennan Manning, says, 'Define yourself radically as one beloved by God. This is the true self. Every other identity is illusion.' How might defining ourselves in this way be different to the three questions above?

The Message translation of Romans 12:1-2 brings out a sense of purpose in life as the author, Paul, explains the concept of 'worship' to his audience:

'So here's what I want you to do, God helping you: Take your everyday, ordinary life – your sleeping, eating, going-to-work, and walking-around life – and place it before God as an offering. Embracing what God does for you is the best thing you can do for him. Don't become so well-adjusted to your culture that you fit into it without even thinking. Instead, fix your attention on God. You'll be changed from the inside out. Readily recognize what he wants from you, and quickly respond to it. Unlike the culture around you, always dragging you down to its level of immaturity, God brings the best out of you, develops well-formed maturity in you.'

Q6 According to the above extract, what ingredients are necessary to live with that kind of purpose?

Q7 What would you expect God to do for you if you lived like that?

TOM'S STORY

I was recently diagnosed with general anxiety disorder, even though I've experienced it since I was 18. I remember getting on a bus and after three stops I suddenly had the urge to get off, feeling like I couldn't continue the journey. I was supposed to be going on an evening out. My friends couldn't understand it and I couldn't explain it. That was when I realised I wasn't well.

At church one time someone went up to the front and said that God said someone here is scared to get on public transport. My friend John was like, 'Tom!' I was like, 'No!' John practically dragged me up front to be prayed for. This guy who had been at the front prayed for me there and then, and since that moment I've never had a problem on public transport again. I got a bus the next day because John was wondering if I could do it. I wasn't sure, but I did it. Suddenly finding that foothold gave me back a sense of control in my life. I'd been given freedom. I had been walking everywhere and I'd lost 2 stone! I was getting back four hours of my life every day.

It's not only about God's help – as important as that is, and he will support you and you can feel his support, that's possible – but God also enables and empowers us to get over our mental ill-health. It can come from God and we need to engage with that and take it on. I don't believe anyone can just click their fingers and be healed. It's a journey I'm on and will be on for the foreseeable future. But I believe God gave me a foothold to get control of my life. Since then I've had all kinds of counselling etc. that has built on that foundation. I lead a pretty much normal life. I can go out when I want, take public transport, hold down a job – before, all these things seemed impossible.

Q8 In the story above, Tom describes God giving him a 'foothold'. What could a foothold look like for you?

Q9 How might putting your life 'before God as an offering', 'embracing what God does for you', fixing 'your attention on God' affect your perspective on your own wellbeing?

Q10 How might that perspective propel you to seek treatment in the following areas?

(a) physical/medical

(b) social/community

(c) spiritual/prayer

(d) psychological/therapeutic

Q11 If you knew that you were on a journey to wholeness and wellbeing, how would that change your approach to life?

Worship is good for us. It flows from a sense of awe and wonder of God, of what he has done, and the life he is drawing us into. Psychologists exploring the positive effects of experiences of 'awe' and 'wonder' conclude that, in a world in which everyone is constantly distracted, 'even brief experiences of awe lead people to feel less narcissistic and entitled, and more attuned to the common humanity [we] share.' [7] Worship isn't just singing, it is an attitude we can adopt towards all of life, as we step out in bold love toward God and others in all we do.

To free you from distraction and free up your mind, could you turn off your phone and computer for an entire day this week? You can use every moment you feel the urge to check for notifications as a trigger to appreciate everything and everyone around you, worshipping God and becoming mindful of the life he is calling you into today. If you decide to do this, why not grab a friend and do this together? You might like to use the translation of Romans 12:1-2 in this study to guide your thoughts. Discuss your experiences the next day (via text, if you have to!).

[7] theguardian.com/lifeandstyle/2017/oct/29/ awe-inspiring-do-moments-of-wonder-make-us- nicer-people

WHERE IS GOD WHEN I DON'T FEEL HIM?

STUDY #9

KEY IDEA

'Wilderness' is a valid part of human (and divine) experience. God is there even if we don't feel him.

KEY PASSAGES

Psalm 38
Mark 1:9-15

Many people experience periods of 'wilderness' in their lives. These are times when they feel emotionally barren, unable to connect to God or other people in a meaningful way. Yet there's no easy explanation for why these seasons come about. Although the Christian tradition holds out the truth that we will somehow, by God's leading, emerge from the wilderness and be stronger for our experience, trite answers and fridge-magnet verses aren't always as comforting as they are intended to be. Often the only hope to cling to is that we are not the first, and we are not alone.

Christianity offers a truth unique among all other philosophies and religions: God himself experienced the wilderness, not only in a desert, but also in a garden. He knows the pain of unanswered prayers and feeling abandoned, even by God! Hanging on a cross, Jesus cried out into the emptiness, *'My God, my God, why have you forsaken me?'* (Matthew 27:46). Christians believe in a God who is able to empathise with us. He sits with us in the dark, and he validates our silence.

Q1 What emotions do you feel towards God at this moment in your life?

Q2 Have you ever had experiences where God felt distant, or you doubted that he was there?

Take some time to soak in Psalm 38.

Q3 Where does reading this poem leave you?

Q4 What kind of imagery resonates or jars with you from this poem?

Q5 Read Psalm 38 again – this time out loud. What strikes you this time?

Q6 Pick two or three words from the poem that capture what it means to you.

Q7 What goodness, beauty or truth can you find here?

Read Mark 1:9-15.

Q8 What do you notice about the state Jesus was in before he went into the wilderness?

Q9 What do you imagine Jesus experienced during his forty days in the wilderness?

Q10 What do you notice about the state Jesus was in after he emerged from the wilderness?

Q11 What lessons might you draw from this for your own situation?

JAMILA'S STORY

I began self-harming around 15. It helped me to maintain the image of a clever, successful, smiley person. I got to university and thought: that was a teenage phase, I'm fine now. But it came back as a way to cope with stress.

As much as I told myself my worth wasn't based on academic success, it was. I was exhausted and miserable all the time, but it wasn't until I stopped eating that I realised I was depressed. I could still function on minimum work requirements, but cooking or facing housemates asking 'How are you?' was just too much.

There were times when I was the most desperate for God I've ever been. It almost felt like this was how it should be. I could cry out and be completely open. 'I've no idea what's going on, I hope you do.' I talked to people in my life about different parts of my life, but God knew all of it, so I might as well tell him how it really was.

But then I also didn't have a sense that God was there. I felt very broken, very sinful, and like God didn't care about me – and why should he anyway when I'm such a mess? And if God doesn't want anything to do with me, then why would I want to have anything to do with him?

Since then, which was a low point, things have been getting better. I feel back to the normal me (and am on a journey to figuring out what that is). But every time I think this is now 'sorted', there are blips.

Something powerful I have learned is that I am even more broken and sinful than I realised. But that God's love and grace is even greater than I hoped. I have experienced God's grace in the practical things – he still works through us no matter how messed up we are. The CU didn't go bankrupt with me as treasurer. I got through my degree. I had conversations with friends about God even when I wasn't sure he was there.

Psalm 139 showed me that even when I don't understand my own head, God does. I am not a speck of dirt; I am a person God made and loves. Wherever I go (physically, mentally or spiritually!) I can't run away from him. Even when life is overwhelming, the Lord is my shepherd.

Q12 What do you make of Jamila's story and her sense of who God is?

One New Testament writer states, '*For Jesus is not some high priest who has no sympathy for our weaknesses and flaws. He has already been tested in every way that we are tested; but He emerged victorious, without failing God. So let us step boldly to the throne of grace, where we can find mercy and grace to help when we need it most.*' (Hebrews 4:15-16, The Voice).

Q13 How do you see Jamila steeping 'boldly to the throne of grace'?

Q14 How might God's mercy and grace be a resource to you, day to day? Can you think of concrete expressions of these things?

In contrast to the promises that we hear from adverts, politicians, educators and even the promises we make to ourselves, God's promises are utterly reliable. His words can be something that brings comfort as a lifeline when we feel adrift. Take a look at the following verses and consider committing one to memory so that you can allow it to soak into your inner life this week. Then ask yourself, what difference has it made?

Matthew 11:28-29

Romans 8:38-39

Philippians 4:6-7

Jude 24-25

HOW CAN I BEGIN TO LOVE MY NEIGHBOUR AS I LOVE MYSELF?

STUDY #10

KEY IDEA

Self-love is not a given but we are called to courageously love others step by step.

KEY PASSAGES

1 John 4
Galatians 6:2

Loving our neighbours can be difficult when we struggle to love ourselves. But, contrary to popular culture, self-love is not something we just muster up or convince ourselves of. That's only ever going to be a failing strategy, because it's so difficult to convince yourself of your own propaganda.

A more robust sense of self-worth and self-love flows out of healthy relationships with others and ultimately with God. If others love me, perhaps I am loveable.

God's radical love frees us to acknowledge our own brokenness without fear we will be found unloveable by him. He took the initiative to invite us into relationship with him not because of anything we had done, but simply because he loves us.

God's total love not only gives us a sense of who we are but also motivates us to love others, showing them the same kind of acceptance that God shows us. It takes patience, it means making ourselves vulnerable, but true life is found when we courageously step out into love for others, just as God did for us.

The actor Martin Sheen said, 'If being pious leads you to a form of personal reflection and acceptance of a higher power, then it has its purpose. But it has to be discarded, in the larger picture, in favor of the community. Because piety is something that you do... alone. And true freedom, spirituality, can only be achieved in community.'[8]

Q1 What do you make of the quote from Martin Sheen, especially what he thinks 'community' is?

Q2 We began this series by looking at Jesus' command to boldly love God with our whole beings and to love our neighbours as ourselves. Do you think it is possible to love God or another person if you struggle to love yourself?

[8]onbeing.org/programs/martin-sheen-spirituality-of-imagination-jun2017/

Take some time to understand the flow of John's thoughts in 1 John 4:7-12.

Q3 How does love fuse together God, us, and one another?

Q4 What fears keep people back from this kind of love?

Q5 How do you react to the idea that love for God and love for one another are inseparable in practice?

Q6 In Galatians 6:2, Paul writes that the church should *'carry each other's burdens, and in this way you will fulfil the law of Christ.'* What do you think this might look like for us?

CS Lewis wrote, 'The load, or weight, or burden of my neighbour's glory should be laid daily on my back, a load so heavy that only humility can carry it, and the backs of the proud will be broken. It is a serious thing to live in a society of possible gods and goddesses, to remember that the dullest most uninteresting person you can talk to may one day be a creature which, if you saw it now, you would be strongly tempted to worship, or else a horror and a corruption such as you now meet, if at all, only in a nightmare. All day long we are, in some degree, helping each other to one or the other of these destinations.[9]

Q7 How does this quote from CS Lewis illustrate what (and how) it means to love your neighbour as yourself?

Q8 Flip the subjects of Lewis' quote around and read it as if your glory should be laid daily on your neighbour's back. What are the implications for you? Making it real: Ava's story (part 2)

[9] CS Lewis, *The Weight of Glory*, p 45 (Zondervan, 2001) (permission pending)

AVA'S STORY
(PART 2)

My friend Hannah who suffers from OCD has really helped me persevere through my anxiety and depression. We don't understand each other's conditions beyond knowing that each other's brain is doing something it shouldn't. Hannah is someone I can phone at any time and say 'I'm thinking this' without having to explain it away or legitimise it. That's so helpful for not getting bogged by thinking 'I'm broken but everyone else is fine'.

Unhelpfully, I don't like to accept help or follow my treatment regime. I'm a 'just get on with it' and 'if everyone thinks you're OK then you're OK' kind of person. But we were never supposed to do this on our own. It goes wrong when you try and shoulder it all yourself. But it's God-honouring and there is joy in seeing people reach out and help one another. That can be anything from a text to a hug, to turning up to cook dinner or doing the shopping. Being present in one another's lives. I'm constantly learning and relearning this.

At some point I need to take responsibility. Other people can't change my mind. They can help and they can point out bad thought patterns, but until I accept who I am as someone God created, I won't see my worth.

I need to engage with this for myself. Also, what am I doing that feeds into that negative view of myself?

For others, it's like helping with any sort of sin. It has to be done in humility. Not that I've got all the answers, but this is what I see. It's so important to communicate an attempt to understand rather than judgement. For me, a big thing that feeds into depression is that I'm not loved or wanted. I have that fear, like most people, that I don't fit in or belong. But I need to take responsibility for those thoughts and put a stop to them. Or be proactive in following people up rather than speculating that they don't love me. It's making myself vulnerable. My husband has been good at reminding me of the objective, external truths that are counter to this. To seek the good things. It's exhausting but necessary!

Q9 To what extent do you resonate with Ava's struggles to help (and be helped by) her friend Hannah?

Q10 Read 1 John 4:7-12 again. This series of studies has pressed into the 'inner life' of a person, but a person always exists in relationship to others. It's impossible to have a healthy inner life without also being in healthy relationships. What kind of communities and friendships are you a part of in which you can bear the burdens of others, and they can bear yours?

Q11 Is there anyone in your life who might benefit from working through these studies with you?

Nothing goes against the grain of our own pride like the practice of serving someone else. Whether it's a lift, making a coffee, doing a shop, walking the long way home so that they can get back safely, or any one of the infinite number of acts that cost us something for the sake of blessing someone else – these moments are powerful opportunities to step into the mindset of Christ (Philippians 2:5-11) and practise the kind of neighbour love that is the expression of a healthy inner life. As a resolution for this week, maybe look out for an opportunity for you to serve someone else and bear their burden for a while.

WHAT AM I REALLY HOPING FOR?

STUDY #11

KEY IDEA

The New Creation captures our imaginations and inspires us to live with hope.

KEY PASSAGES

Revelation 21
Revelation 22:1-5

Everyone experiences a disconnect between who they are and who they wish that they could be. That's normal. So perhaps a more interesting question is, who do you imagine your future self to be?

The Bible gives a vision of the future that is a re-creation of all that God originally made good. It's the completion of all the potential that was embedded in the world God created. And, as creatures of that world, we too will be brought to full completion.

John's vision in Revelation is designed to inspire the readers in the midst of their here-and-now lives as they face persecution and struggles, perhaps wondering if God is really present. It is a vision that is meant to fuel the believer's hope in a God who overcomes all brokenness and evil and calls us to persevere in the midst of struggle.

Q1 What do you imagine your future to be like? You might like to think in terms of

(a) your inner life

(b) your relationships

(c) your purpose

Take some time to read about the vision of the future that John captures in Revelation 21:1-8 and 22:1-5. Note what strikes you and where you have questions.

Q2 Imagine the scene of Jesus wiping away tears from the eyes of his people. What do you think this is about?

Q3 What do you think it means to have a 'new' inner life?

Q4 What do you think it means to have access to 'the spring of the water of life'?

Q5 Where do you notice echoes of the Garden of Eden? Why might this be significant?

Q6 How do you react to the idea that God will dwell among people?

Q7 What difference do you think John wanted his vision to make to his readers?

NAOMI'S STORY
(PART 2)

The main thing that happened at university was that I found Jesus. But that just meant finding a standard to fail by. The underlying 'everyone hates me' just got stronger and out of control. I hated myself. I was unable to sleep and afraid of the dark. I didn't feel safe. Night anxiety is still a struggle for me.

At university, my main (outward) coping strategy was to assume that this is the way the world is, so this is the way I am. Secretly, I took pills. Another coping mechanism was to manipulate relationships to avoid unconditional love. Any friend that questioned any of my decisions, I rejected. Then I had no friends. I was on painkillers and I overdosed. The idea that God created me and this world made me so angry! You just see the brokenness and you can't see any joy or redemption coming through. Change was also a coping mechanism because you can remain at the surface level.

I had a year out, then came to Trent and found a mentor through the Navigators. This blew my mind because there was a level of engagement with brokenness but a stronger sense of hope, which is a big word for me at the moment.

I recently gave someone an image: My friend, who was horrendously depressed, was in a completely black room. Jesus was sitting next to her. She couldn't see him. She needed to be reminded that he was there. That's different to Jesus being the light and coming in to fix everything now. God is with us in the pain; he sees it and suffers it.

An amazing thing God gave us is our imagination. I think he wants us to use our minds to create a better world. We can imagine things going well and think of new ways of living because we have these massive imaginations. I often use mine to create negative possibilities of worlds I don't want to live in. But I am able to imagine that I can sleep safely and people care about me – that is something huge that God gave us. It's a New Creation tool. I think God wants us to take time to engage with all the information we're processing all the time, to pay attention and live reflectively.

Q8 Naomi describes her imagination as a 'New Creation' tool. Do you find your imagination is a tool for good or bad in your life?

The theologian Walter Brueggemann writes, '[Hope] flies in the face of all those claims we have been told are facts. Hope is the refusal to accept the reading of reality which is the majority opinion… Hope is subversive… daring to announce that the present to which we have all made commitments is now called into question.'[10]

Q9 Look at the Revelation passages again. If you were living in that city, what would these things look like?

(a) your inner life

(b) your relationships

(c) your purpose

Q10 What difference could this vision make to how you imagine your best possible future? What can you do to move towards it?

[10] Walter Brueggemann, *The Prophetic Imagination* (Fortress Press, 2001)

To be human is to be creative. You may not consider yourself an artist or musician, but there are plenty of ways that every single person can create: artworks, conversations, meals, designs, outfits, moments. And God loves to see what we create (Genesis 2:19).

Our creativity, fueled by our imagination, reveals what we think is important. At its best, our creativity embodies our hope for a better world and it brings that hope to others. The people we know (and those we don't) can be blessed by our creativity. This week, why not make time for something creative? You could try…

- Cooking a meal
- Writing a song
- Starting a new conversation
- Redecorating a room
- Writing a poem
- Reading a book to someone
- Giving a friend the space to talk
- Making someone a present

…or anything that brings a hint of the New Creation to your world and relationships. It needn't be perfect (God's glory shines through imperfection) but you might just get a hint of the kingdom coming, on earth as it is in heaven.

PERSONAL REFLECTION AND NEXT STEPS

'I know God is with me as I start the next chapter to my life. I know the tendency towards depressive thoughts will always be a weakness for me and it will be the first point of attack, it's how I'm wired. But I am much more willing to call out lies and I can reach out and ask for help or prayer. I am living more vulnerably now.' (Katy)

'It's OK to feel miserable but it's not OK to stay in that place. Find people to talk it out with. Invest in some real life, gritty, conversational relationships. Don't hide in Netflix, alcohol, coffee etc. Be prepared to do hard stuff.' (Priya)

During the next week, take some time on your own to reflect on the following questions. Then, make some time to process your answers with someone you trust. Flip back to your answers to Q1 and Q2 in Study 1 and reflect on your journey as you have explored what makes for a healthy inner life.

Q1 At this point, what do you think a healthy mind makes possible?

Q2 Going forward, how will what you believe affect your inner wellbeing, and how will your inner wellbeing affect your beliefs about yourself, others and God?

Q3 Read Mark 12:28-34, the first passage mentioned in this series of studies. What does this mean to you now?

Q4 Who might be able to journey with you as you pursue a healthier inner life? How could you support each other?